Making Great Works in Bronze

by Myka-Lynne Sokoloff

Harcourt
SCHOOL PUBLISHERS

Cover, ©Christie's Images/SuperStock; p.3, ©Erich Lessing/Art Resource, NY; p.3, ©Erich Lessing/Art Resource, NY;p.4, ©Vince Bucci/Getty Images; p.4,©DigitalVues/Alamy; p.5, ©David McNew/Getty Images; p.5, ©David McNew/Getty Images; p.6,©The Art Archive/Archaeological Museum Delphi/Dagli Orti; p.7, ©Scala/Art Resource, NY; p.9, ©The Art Archive / Dagli Ortip.8, ©Jim Zuckerman/CORBIS; p.10, ©Alinari Archives/CORBIS; p.12, ©The Philadelphia Museum of Art/Art Resource, NY; p.13,©Cummer Museum of Art & Gardens/SuperStock; p.14, ©Rudi Von Briel/PhotoEdit

Printed in China

ISBN 10: 0-15-351651-8
ISBN 13: 978-0-15-351651-1

Ordering Options
ISBN 10: 0-15-351215-6 (Grade 5 Advanced Collection)
ISBN 13: 978-0-15-351215-5 (Grade 5 Advanced Collection)
ISBN 10: 0-15-358144-1 (package of 5)
ISBN 13: 978-0-15-358144-1 (package of 5)

5 6 7 8 9 10   468   12 11 10 09

The "Lost Wax" Process

What do ancient Greece, the Italian Renaissance, Africa, France, and the Wild West have in common? One answer is the "lost wax" process. Lost wax describes a process that artists have used around the world. Scholars trace its use back thousands of years.

An ornamental bronze ▶
axe from Austria

▲ Bronze Age tools and weapons

The Casting Process

1 A form is made of clay or plaster.

2 The form is heated, and the wax melts.

The lost wax process is used to make items from bronze. Bronze is a metal alloy made by mixing copper and tin at extremely high temperatures. Making bronze was once so important that an entire period of history is known as the Bronze Age. Different parts of the world went through a Bronze Age at different times. The first one began in the Middle East about 3500 B.C. At first, bronze was mostly used to make tools and weapons. Later, it was also used for art objects. Many of these treasures from around the world still exist.

③ Bronze is poured in to fill the space.

④ The clay layers are removed.

The lost wax process follows a lengthy procedure. **❶** The first step is to make a clay model of the object you want to create. (Sometimes plaster is used instead of clay.) Next, the model is dipped in hot wax and cooled. Then, another layer of clay is added over the wax layer. **❷** The entire object is heated to a high enough temperature to melt the wax. The melted wax drips out through holes in the clay. **❸** Melted bronze is poured into the space where the wax had been. **❹** Once the bronze hardens, both layers of clay are removed, and the bronze figure remains.

The *Charioteer of Delphi*

One of the most famous statues of ancient Greece was made using the lost wax process. The artist is unknown. The sculpture is called the *Charioteer of Delphi* and shows a young man who has just won a horse race. His lifelike eyes are made of a black stone called onyx. His eyelids and mouth are made of copper. The headband is formed from silver. The rest of the statue is made of bronze. Part of the statue is long gone. When it was made, it also included four horses.

The statue was finished around 478 B.C. It was well-preserved because it was buried in the ground. It was found at Delphi, one of the most important places in ancient Greece.

Delphi was thought to be the center of the earth in ancient times. People came from all over Greece to ask questions of the oracle, a very wise person. Today tourists visit Delphi for its natural beauty and its importance in Greek history. They also come to see the *Charioteer* and other ancient works of art.

Doors of Paradise

Nearly all visitors to Florence, Italy, visit the piazza, or square, around a large church called the *Duomo*, which means "cathedral" in Italian. One of the things they go to see at the square is a set of doors comprised of bronze sculptures.

A competition was held in A.D. 1401 to decide who would design these doors. An artist named Ghiberti won the competition and worked for twenty years to complete them. Ghiberti used the lost-wax process to make all twenty-eight bronze panels that are displayed on the doors.

The *Duomo*

    The artist who lost the contest was named Brunelleschi. He was so angry about losing the contest that he left Florence for many years. He went off to Rome, where he rediscovered the ancient art of making cement. He would use this knowledge when he returned to Florence. He later had the job of building a huge cement dome for the church that now gives the square its name, *Piazza del Duomo*.

Ghiberti's doors were finally completed in A.D. 1452, the same year that Leonardo da Vinci was born. At this point, Ghiberti was asked to design two more doors.
It took twenty-four more years to design and cast these doors. Each panel of the doors shows a religious story.

Ghiberti had many helpers in casting the doors. He was required to make the trees himself, as well as the hair and faces of the people. The later pair of doors shows the changing style of art at the time. The proportions of the people were more like those in real life than they had been on the earlier doors. The artist Michelangelo thought the doors were so perfect that he named them the *Doors of Paradise*.

A panel from the *Doors of Paradise*

Leonardo's Horse

Leonardo da Vinci learned how to cast bronze from his teacher, Verrocchio. Verrocchio died at a time when he was trying to successfully complete a bronze casting of a huge horse. Later Leonardo learned that the Duke of Milan wanted a large horse statue. Leonardo could easily envision the giant bronze work of art.

Although Leonardo did not specialize as a sculptor, he was the right person for the job. He began work on his horse in 1489. He chose parts of several real horses as models for his statue. He studied how horses used their muscles when they moved. A man of many interests, Leonardo got a bit sidetracked. He created designs for machines to feed horses and clean their stables, hundreds of years ahead of his time.

Leonardo's sketches of his horse

After a few years of work, the huge, clay horse statue was ready for casting, but the bronze for casting the horse was gone! When a war broke out between Milan and France, the bronze was used to make cannons. In fact, the French even used the clay model for target practice. Like his teacher, Leonardo was never able to bring his bronze horse sculpture to life.

African Gold Weights

While Renaissance artists were using lost wax to cast bronze in Europe, metal workers in western Africa had been doing the same thing for centuries. They used this method to make gold weights.

African gold weights were actually made of bronze. They were called gold weights because of their use. Gold was not shaped into bricks or coins for trade in Africa. Gold dust was used in place of money. Traders used scales to measure the dust. Gold dust was placed on one side of a tiny scale and gold weights were placed on the other side.

There were two main styles of gold weights. In one style, weights were made in simple shapes, such as cubes and pyramids. The other style included shapes that looked like real objects. Some of these looked like vegetables; others were shaped like animals or people.

Fathers gave sets of gold weights to their sons when the sons married. The weights were a tool that would help the sons earn a living.

The Thinker

Quick! Get into a thinking pose. Now if you look in the mirror, you might find yourself making the same gesture as one of the most famous statues in the world. The statue, called *The Thinker*, was made using the lost wax process. The first casting of this sculpture was made in 1902. Since then, the sculpture has been cast over twenty times, and the castings are housed in museums around the world.

The French sculptor, Auguste Rodin, lived from 1840 to 1917. He was well-known for creating many large statues. Some were made using the lost wax process. Others were carved from marble.

Frederic Remington

Cowboys in the old West worked the open range on horseback. Can you picture how they might have looked? Chances are the image in your mind looks a lot like cowboy statues made by Frederic Remington.

Remington was born in the United States in 1861, and he lived until 1909. He had many talents and resisted limiting himself to one field of work.

Remington was both a writer and an artist. He wrote magazine articles and books, mostly about the Wild West. His illustrations appeared in the most popular magazines of his day. One time, Remington drew a picture of a cowboy for a magazine article. The writer of the article was Teddy Roosevelt, the man who would become the twenty-sixth United States President.

Remington turned to making bronze sculptures in 1895. Most of his sculptures were made using the lost wax process. His first statue, a bronze work completed that same year he began using the process, is called the *Bronco Buster*. This statue now sits in the White House.

Thousands of years ago, people discovered how to make bronze. This knowledge would help them make tools that they could use for farming and building. Humans have greater needs than simple food and shelter, though. Once those needs are satisfied, people seek more. Many turn to art. Knowledge of the lost wax method led many cultures to begin using bronze to create art. This process has given us some of the most beloved artworks known today.

The Alice in Wonderland Monument. Sculpted by Jose de Creeft, 1959, Central Park, New York City

Think Critically

1. List the works of art and their artists described in this book in chronological order by the year they were completed.

2. Which work described in the book shows the best example of teamwork? Explain your answer.

3. What was the author's main purpose in writing this book?

4. In what way are the African gold weights different from the other objects described in the book?

5. If you could own one of the objects described in this book, which one would you choose? Give reasons for your choice.

 **Social Studies**

Other Great Artists Do some research on the Internet or use other library resources to learn more about one of the artists mentioned in this book other than Leonardo da Vinci. Write a short biography, including information about some of the artist's famous pieces of art.

School-Home Connection Tell members of your family about the lost wax process and some objects that have been made using this method. Then ask family members to describe statues they have seen.

Word Count: 1,492